HALLOWEEN COOKBOOK

65 Halloween Recipes For A Scary & Tasty Halloween!

By
Katya Johansson

TABLE OF CONTENTS

1. Tasty Web Cake 1
2. Chocolate Tart 4
3. Amazing Beetroot drinks 7
4. Amazing Dead scones 8
5. Amazing Zombie Fingers 11
6. Tasty Maggoty Apples 12
7. Eyeball Tail 14
8. Frozen Tasty Banana Phantoms 15
9. Amazing Red Velvet Cake 16
10. Bat Chocolate Rolls 19
11. Amazing Cupcakes 21
12. Tasty Caption Treats 23
13. Funny Face Tasty Treats 25
13. Slime Bug Wonderful Cups 27
14. Sausage Mummy Delicious scoops 28
15. Best Witch's Cauldron 30
16. Dracula's Tasty Punch 32
17. Eerie eyeball pops 33
18. Tasty Halloween jam 34
19. Healthy Orange Pumpkin Treats 36
20. Haunted Cemetery Cake 38
21. Chocolate Creepy Crawly Treats 41
22. Tasty Eyeball pasta 42
23. Delicious Spider Chocolate Biscuits 43
24. Chocolate Arachnid Tasty Jams 45
25. Pumpkin Witch Delicious Cupcakes 47
26. Amazing Mummy Hot Dogs 49
27. Amazing Deviled Eggs 51
28. Healthy Pumpkin Cake 53
29. Amazing Pumpkin Cookies 57
30. Amazing Goblin Flatbreads 59
31. Amazing Halloween Ghosties 60
32. Amazing Cauldron Curry 61
33. Monster Fingers with Cheese Paws 63
34. Amazing Guacamole with Black Beans 64
35. Wonderful Monster Mucus 65
36. Healthy Spinach Ricotta Skulls 66
37. Amazing Spiderweb Eggs 68

38. Halloween Peas 69
39. Wonderful Cured Epidermis 71
40. Wonderful Bat Wings 72
41. Squeamish Squash and Tasty Rice 74
42. Tasty Potatoes and Romesco Sauce 75
43. French Onion Soups 77
44. Wonderful Worms in Dirt 79
45. Best Pickled Brains 80
46. Spicy Tasty Bat Wings 81
47. Wonderful Ghastly Ghoulash 82
48. Amazing Recipe 84
49. Ghost Sandwiches 85
50. Eye Catching Soup 86
51. Tasty Creature Chips 88
52. Grilled Cheese Tasty Sandwiches 89
53. Amazing Fingers and Toes 90
54. Petrified Cheese Log 92
55. Halloween Cheese Crackers 93
56. Devils on Wonderful Horseback 94
57. Amazing Tacos 95
58. Amazing Spider Deviled Eggs 96
59. Amazing Mummy Dogs 97
60. Halloween Fingers 98
61. Roasted Healthy Pumpkin Seeds 100
62. Halloween Tasty Fondue 101
63. Amazing Yoda Soda 103
64. Apple with Cheese Spread 104
65. Apple and Blue Cheese Spread 105

HALLOWEEN COOKBOOK

For the chocolate ganache

- 100g dim chocolate
- 50ml twofold cream
- 25g margarine
- To serve
- pinch of flaky ocean salt
- red and pink solidified flower petals (shop purchased or make your own, see tip)

Method

1. Begin by making the baked good. Cream the margarine and sugar in a huge bowl, utilizing an electric whisk or a wooden spoon, until pale and light. Include the egg yolks, each one in turn, beating great after every option, then include the vanilla seeds. Blend in the flour, then unite the mixture with your hands until it frames a ball that leaves the bowl clean. Wrap in stick film and chill for 30 mins or overnight.
2. Warm stove to 190C/170C fan/gas 5 and oil a 23cm free bottomed, profound fluted tart tin. Daintily clean your work surface with flour, then reveal the chilled baked good and line your tin with it, ensuring there's a slight shade. On the off chance that the baked good tears, utilize your fingers to push the pieces back together (it will meld back perfectly in the stove). Put a bit of baking material on top of the baked good and measure it down with baking beans. Heat for 15 mins, evacuate the material and beans, and come back to the broiler for a further 15 mins until fresh and brilliant.
3. Trim any abundance cake with a serrated blade, so the edge sits flush with the tin, and let cool totally.

Copyright © 2016 – All Rights Reserved | Katya Johansson

KATYA JOHANSSON

4. Blend all the rose and cassis layer Ingredients in a bowl, utilizing enough food shading to turn it dim pink. Empty the blend into the baked good case and chill for 10 mins to solidify.
5. In the meantime, for the cheesecake layer, break the chocolate into pieces and tip into an large, heatproof bowl. In a little container, tenderly warmth the twofold cream and cream cheddar until sizzling and dissolved together. Rapidly pour the blend over the chocolate, let it sit for 1 min, then mix until totally smooth and dissolved. Pour the blend over the rose and cassis layer, then give back the tart to the cooler.
6. To make the chocolate ganache, put all the ganache Ingredients in a heatproof bowl and microwave in short blasts until dissolved. (Then again, warm every one of the Ingredients in a bowl over a skillet of scarcely stewing water.) Pour over the cheesecake layer and chill the tart for no less than 30 mins, or overnight in the event that you favor. Just before serving, painstakingly expel the tart from the tin and put on a serving plate or board. Adorn with a pinch of ocean salt pieces and a couple flower petals. Cut into cuts and serve.

HALLOWEEN COOKBOOK

1. TASTY WEB CAKE

INGREDIENTS

FOR THE CAKE

- 110g unsalted spread, in addition to additional for lubing
- 3 tbsp cocoa powder
- 140ml chocolate strong (we utilized Young's Double Chocolate Stout, accessible from Tesco)
- 170g white caster sugar
- 170g light brown delicate sugar
- 1 tsp vanilla concentrate
- 3 large eggs, softly beaten
- 100g dull chocolate, softened and cooled
- 280g plain flour
- 2 tsp bicarbonate of pop

FOR THE WHITE CHOCOLATE BUTTERCREAM

- 3 large egg whites
- 240g caster sugar
- 360g unsalted spread, room temperature
- 200g white chocolate, liquefied and cooled
- 100g white smaller than normal marshmallows
- 25g dark sugar glue

Copyright © 2016 – All Rights Reserved | Katya Johansson

KATYA JOHANSSON

METHOD

1. Warm stove to 180C/160C fan/gas 4. Oil three 20cm round cake tins and line the bases with baking material. To make the cake, put the cocoa in a bowl, and include 280ml boiling water and race until broke down. Pour in the strong, blend, then put aside to cool.
2. In a stand blender or a large bowl utilizing an electric hand whisk, beat together the margarine, both sugars and vanilla concentrate until light and fleecy (around 5 mins). Include the eggs little by small, blending until completely fused before including more. When all the egg has been included, spoon in the liquefied chocolate and blend to consolidate.
3. In another bowl, blend the flour, bicarb and 1/2 tsp salt. Add this blend to the margarine blend in three phases, rotating with the hefty blend (which will be extremely runny). Pour the player similarly between the readied tins and heat for 25-30 mins until a stick embedded into the cake tells the truth. Leave to cool in the tins for 10 mins, then turn out onto a wire rack to cool totally.
4. To make the buttercream, put the egg whites and sugar in a heatproof bowl and set over a skillet of tenderly stewing water. Mix with a speed until the sugar has broken down and the blend is warm to the touch. Expel the bowl from the warmth and beat with an electric hand speed on rapid until the blend has tripled in volume and has chilled off. Gradually include the margarine 1 tbsp. at once while keeping on whisking. When all the spread has been included, the blend ought to look gleaming and thick – on the off chance that it doesn't, continue speeding until it does, or if the bowl still feels warm, chill

Copyright © 2016 – All Rights Reserved | Katya Johansson

2. CHOCOLATE TART

INGREDIENTS

FOR THE BAKED GOOD

- 100g margarine
- 75g brilliant caster sugar
- 3 egg yolks
- 1 vanilla case, seeds as it were
- 200g plain flour, in addition to additional for tidying

FOR THE ROSE AND CASSIS LAYER

- 3 tbsp twofold cream
- 3 tbsp Crème de Cassis
- 1/4 tsp rosewater
- 250g icing sugar
- a couple drops pink food shading

FOR THE CHEESECAKE LAYER

- 100g dim chocolate
- 100g milk chocolate
- 75ml twofold cream
- 150g full-fat cream cheddar

HALLOWEEN COOKBOOK

for 10 mins before whisking once more. When prepared, blend in the softened white chocolate.

5. To gather the cake, put one of the cake layers on a cake stand and top with a layer of buttercream. Rehash with the other two layers. Spread the rest of the buttercream everywhere throughout the cake, utilizing a spatula or palette blade to smooth the sides. Chill for 1 hr. or until the buttercream is firm (see tip, underneath).

6. To enrich, soften the marshmallows in a heatproof bowl set over a skillet of stewing water, mixing every once in a while. Expel from the warmth and put to the other side for a couple of mins until the blend is sufficiently cool to handle. Utilize your fingers to get a little measure of the marshmallow and extend it to frame long strands (plunging your fingers in vegetable or sunflower oil will!) Drape the strands over the cake in an arbitrary example, so it's completely covered. Make an insect utilizing the sugar glue (move two balls, one greater than the other, for the body, and thin strands for the legs) and place on top of the cake. Will keep for up to three days in a water/air proof container.

3. Amazing Beetroot Drinks

Ingredients

For the beetroot lemonade

- 200g crude beetroot
- juice 8 lemons
- 200g brilliant caster sugar

For the mixed drink

- 300ml Aperol
- ice
- 750ml Prosecco

Method

1. To start with, make the beetroot lemonade. In a bowl, blend together the beetroot, lemon squeeze and sugar. Soak in the ice chest for no less than 1 hr., mixing once in a while to break up the sugar. Pour the blend through a strainer into an large container to dispose of the mash.
2. To make the mixed drink, pour 25ml of the beetroot lemonade into every glass, trailed by 50ml of Aperol and a couple ice 3D squares. Best with Prosecco and serve.

4. Amazing Dead scones

Ingredients

For the scones

- 175g cool marginally salted margarine, cubed
- 250g plain flour, in addition to additional for cleaning
- 100g icing sugar
- 1 substantial egg yolk
- 500g imperial icing sugar, in addition to a little to dust
- 500g pack set white sugar paste or fondant icing

Method

1. To make the mixture, tip the margarine, flour and a decent pinch of salt into a food processor. Mix until the blend takes after breadcrumbs, and the margarine is very much blended in. Include the icing sugar, egg yolk and 2 tsp cool water. Mix again until the blend begins to cluster together, include another 1 tsp water if the batter looks excessively dry, yet have a go at, making it impossible to abstain from including any more, as this will make the scones intense. Tip the morsels out onto a work surface and squash everything together to make a bundle of mixture, you may need to manipulate it a couple times for an even surface. Wrap in stick film, pat into a level plate and chill for 30 mins.

HALLOWEEN COOKBOOK

2. Warm broiler to 180C/160C fan/gas 4 and line 2 large baking sheets with baking material. On the off chance that the mixture is firm, abandon it at room temperature for 10 mins, or until mellowed a bit. Tidy your work surface with flour, then unwrap and reveal the batter to the thickness of a £1 coin. Stamp out the greatest number of skull shapes as you can, then squash the scraps of batter back together, reroll and stamp out a couple of something beyond. Organize the skull shapes over the plate, prepare for 18-20 mins, until simply brilliant, swapping the plate over part of the way through if your stove cooks unevenly. Leave to cool on the plate for 10 mins, then exchange to wire racks to cool totally.
3. While the rolls cool, set up the icing. In a huge bowl, blend the regal icing sugar with enough water to make a thick icing. Separate the icing into the same number of dishes as the quantity of hues you'd get a kick out of the chance to utilize (you'll have to shading 1 group dark for the mouth) then utilize the food shading to shading each a clear shade - a minor drop of the food shading glue goes far, so begin with somewhat, then include increasingly in the event that you like. On the off chance that the icing is too thick to pipe, include a drop more water. Exchange every shading to a different dispensable funneling sack and secure the closures (garments pegs benefit work of keeping the finishes shut.)
4. Sever 50g of the sugar paste and put the rest aside, wrapped in clingfilm (This will keep it from drying out and breaking.) Use the red food shading to color the little piece of sugar paste red, manipulating until equally hued. To make the roses, take hazelnut-sized chunks of the red sugar paste, and squeeze them into long thin oval shapes on the work surface (about 1cm x 4 cm, utilize a bit of icing sugar at first glance on the off chance that it gets excessively sticky.) Roll up the sugar paste from one

end to make a rose. While still on its side, remove the base to give you a level base. Proceed with whatever is left of the red sugar paste until you have around 20 roses (enough for 4 bread rolls.)

5. Clean down the surface, and tidy with somewhat additional icing sugar. Reveal the rest of the sugar paste to the thickness of a 50p piece, then cut out the same number of skull shapes as you have scones. Utilize a tad bit of one of the shaded icings to stick the sugar paste skulls to the bread rolls.

6. Scrunch any sugar paste scraps back together and color the chunk of sugar paste dark with the dark food shading, massaging until you have an even shading. Reveal the dark sugar paste and stamp out circles for the eyes (utilize a round cutter, or the end of a funneling spout.) Stick the eyes and roses to the bread rolls with a tad bit of the shaded illustrious icing. Clip off the side of all the funneling sacks to make a modest opening and improve the bread rolls as you wish – blooms, hearts and dotty outlines all look great. Leave the bread rolls to dry for 1 hr. before serving. The enlivened scones will keep for 3 days in a fixed container.

5. Amazing Zombie Fingers

Ingredients

- 250g stoned dates
- 100g dim chocolate, hacked
- 3 tbsp smooth nutty spread
- 3 tbsp porridge oats
- chipped toasted almonds

Method

1. Tip every one of the Ingredients aside from the almonds into a food processor and heartbeat until you have a rubbly looking blend.
2. Line a plate with baking material and shape the blend into fingers, then lay them on the plate. Press an almond "fingernail" into the end of every finger and place in the ice chest to solidify for no less than 1 hr. Serve jabbing out of a bowl.

KATYA JOHANSSON

6. Tasty Maggoty Apples

Ingredients

- 6 apples
- (we utilized Braeburn)
- juice ½ lemon
- 100g white chocolate
- 50g puffed rice
- jam worm desserts (Optional)

Method

1. Core the apples, beginning at the base and attempting to keep the stalk closes in place. Utilize a limit table blade or melon hotshot to scoop out any outstanding bits of seeds and center on the off chance that you have to. You can likewise utilize a metal stick to make 1 or 2 gaps in the sides. Brush the cut parts of the apples with lemon squeeze and put on a plate or board.
2. Put the chocolate in a heatproof bowl over a dish of stewing water to liquefy. Once dissolved, mix in the puffed rice, then expel from the warmth. Utilizing a teaspoon, pack the chocolate and puffed rice blend into the apples, staying a couple into the littler gaps and on the top to seem as though they're slithering out. Exchange the apples to the ice chest for around 20 mins to set.

Copyright © 2016 – All Rights Reserved | Katya Johansson

HALLOWEEN COOKBOOK

3. Spoon any residual blend into a smaller than usual biscuit tin fixed with paper petit four cases and put in the refrigerator to set alongside the apples.
4. Once the chocolate has set, peel away the paper cases and put the 'larva balls' around the apples. Include a couple of wriggly jam worms as well, in the event that you set out.

KATYA JOHANSSON

9. Amazing Red Velvet Cake

Ingredients

For the Red Velvet Cake

- 175g delicate margarine
- 225g white caster sugar
- 1 tsp vanilla concentrate
- 3 large eggs
- 1 tbsp red food shading glue (we utilized Christmas red from Sugarflair)
- 200g plain flour
- 50g cocoa powder (we utilized Green and Black's)
- 1½ tsp bicarbonate of pop?
- ½ tsp baking powder
- ¼ tsp salt
- 150g pot low-fat plain yogurt, slackened with 2 tbsp milk

For the Fingers and Icing

- around 3 x 114g boxes white chocolate fingers (we discovered them in Tesco)
- 140g icing sugar
- 2 tsp milk
- little blob of red food shading glue
- 100g delicate margarine

HALLOWEEN COOKBOOK

- 300g full-fat cream cheddar, ice chest frosty (we utilized Philadelphia as it has the firmest surface)
- pizzazz 1 orange

Method

1. Warm broiler to 180C/160C fan/gas 4. For the cake, oil 2 x 20cm sandwich tins and line the bases with baking material. Cream together the margarine, sugar and vanilla, then include the eggs, each one in turn, beating great after every egg, until feathery and light. Beat in the shading.
2. Blend the dry elements for the cake, and filter half onto the creamed blend. Overlap in with a spatula, trailed by half of the diminished yogurt. Rehash, then spoon the smooth hitter into the tins and level. Prepare for 25 mins or until risen and springy when squeezed delicately in the inside. Cool for 10 mins, then turn out onto a wire rack and cool totally.
3. For the fingers, line a baking plate with material. Cut one end from every chocolate finger. Blend 50g icing sugar, the milk and a little blob of shading to make a thick, red icing. The icing should be thick to stay put; include somewhat more sugar in the event that you have to. Dunk the disjoined bread closes into the icing, let the abundance dribble off, then paint a red fingernail on the flip side, utilizing a little paintbrush. Leave to dry on the material.
4. For the icing, utilize an electric blender to beat the spread well until exceptionally smooth, then beat in the cream cheddar and the pizzazz (if utilizing) until even. Filter in the rest of the icing sugar, then overlay it into

the cheddar blend utilizing a spatula until smooth. Don't overbeat. Chill until required.
5. Sandwich and cover the top and sides of the cake with the icing – you will just need a thin layer on the sides of the cake to stick on the chocolate fingers. Stand the disjoined fingers around the cake in a flawless neckline, squeezing them daintily into the icing. You'll have a couple left over to put on the top. Keep the cake in the cooler however appreciate it at room temperature.

HALLOWEEN COOKBOOK

10. Bat Chocolate Rolls

Ingredients

- 125g spread
- 85g icing sugar
- 1 huge egg yolk
- 1 tsp vanilla concentrate
- 1 tsp milk
- 175g plain flour, in addition to additional for rolling
- 1 tsp fine espresso-style powder coffee (I utilized Azeera)
- 50g cocoa powder
- ¼ tsp salt
- 100g bar dull or milk chocolate
- chocolate hundreds and thousands
- shaded written work icing (or make your own with 100g icing sugar, 3-4 tsp water and some shading)

Method

1. Warm broiler to 180C/160C fan/gas 4 and line two baking sheets with baking material. Beat the spread and sugar together until velvety and pale, then beat in the yolk, the vanilla and milk. Filter the flour, coffee, cocoa and salt into the bowl, then combine to make a delicate mixture. Shape the mixture into a plate, wrap and chill for 15 mins.
2. Clean the batter done with a little flour, then move it between two huge sheets of baking material, to the

Copyright © 2016 – All Rights Reserved | Katya Johansson

KATYA JOHANSSON

thickness of a £1 coin. Expel the top layer of the paper, stamp shapes with a 8cm bat (or other) cutter, and painstakingly lift to the lined sheets utilizing a palette cut. Re-roll the trimmings. Cut a 1.5cm x 5mm score at the base of every bat's body. This is about right to sit the bats on thick tumblers; if your glasses are better edged, make the steps more slender so that the bats stay put. Heat for 10 mins or until the bread rolls feel sandy and notice rich and chocolatey. Cool on the sheets for 5 mins, then lift the treats onto a wire rack and cool totally.

3. To improve, soften the chocolate over a skillet of stewing water or in the microwave. One roll at once, brush chocolate over the bat ears and wings with a little paintbrush, then cover with chocolate sprinkles. Tap off the overabundance. Pipe appearances and teeth onto your bats, then leave to dry. Keep in a sealed shut container for up to a week.

HALLOWEEN COOKBOOK

11. Amazing Cupcakes

Ingredients

For the cupcakes

- 200g delicate spread
- 175g brilliant caster sugar
- 250g flour
- 1 tsp baking powder
- ¼ tsp salt
- 3 substantial eggs
- ½ tsp vanilla concentrate
- 100ml milk

To Garnish

- 300g icing sugar, filtered
- 2-3 tbsp. milk
- Green food shading glue
- 36 small marshmallows, 12 cut down the middle (for the eyes)
- container of dark channeling icing or gel

Method

KATYA JOHANSSON

1. Warm stove to 180C/160C fan/gas 4 and line a 12-gap biscuit tin with profound biscuit cases. Cream the spread with the sugar until pale and cushioned. Include the rest of the cake Ingredients and beat until smooth. Spoon into the biscuit cases and prepare for 20 mins or until brilliant and a stick embedded into one of the center cakes tells the truth. Cool for 5 mins in the tin, then totally on a wire rack.
2. Utilizing a little, sharp serrated blade, cut a semi-hover bit of cake from the left and right of every cake, to make ventured edges, level with the cupcake case. Next, make a cut around 3cm from the top of the cake, around 1cm profound. Cut a 5mm piece off the surface of the cake to meet this cut, to make a level, raised face and conspicuous temple. Chill for 10 mins to firm the scraps.
3. Blend the icing sugar, milk and green shading to make a thick icing that streams gradually from the spoon. Spoon 1 tbsp onto a cake and let it start to spread itself over the cut shape. Ease it here and there with a palette blade to coat. Include marshmallow neck jolts and eyes. Rehash for every cupcake. Leave to set, then pipe on the appearances and hair.

HALLOWEEN COOKBOOK

12. Tasty Caption Treats

Ingredients

For the treats

- 175g delicate margarine
- 100g brilliant caster sugar
- 1 vast egg yolk
- ½ tsp vanilla concentrate
- pizzazz 1 lemon
- 250g plain flour, in addition to additional for rolling
- ½ tsp salt

To finish

- cake pop sticks
- 200g icing sugar, filtered
- 1 substantial egg white
- food shading of your decision, we utilized orange and pink

Method

1. Beat together the spread and sugar until pale and velvety, then beat in the yolk, vanilla and get-up-and-go. Filter the flour and salt into the bowl, then mix into

Copyright © 2016 – All Rights Reserved | Katya Johansson

KATYA JOHANSSON

make a delicate mixture. Part into two level circles, then wrap in stick film and chill for 30 mins, or until firm however not shake hard. In the interim, warm broiler to 180C/160C fan/gas 4. Line two baking sheets with baking material.

2. Flour the work surface, then roll the mixture to the thickness of 2 x £2 coins. Stamp hovers with an 8cm cutter and re-roll the trimmings. On the off chance that you like, pinch a discourse bubble point into the base of each round. Chill for 10 mins, or until firm, then jab cake pop sticks deliberately into the batter. (I discover putting one hand on top of the batter as I embed the stay with alternate keeps the stick from popping through the surface of the mixture.)

3. Prepare for 12 mins, until pale brilliant. Leave on the plate for 5 mins before lifting to a wire rack (utilize a palette cut instead of the sticks) and cooling totally. Make the icing by beating sugar and egg white until thick and smooth. Expel half to another bowl, shading it, then spoon into a dispensable channeling pack and clip off the tip (or utilize a number 2 spout). Pipe a discourse bubble fringe around every treat and leave to set for a couple of mins.

4. Presently relax the white icing with a couple drops of water until runny. Spoon a little onto every treat and let it surge to the framework, bumping it up to the edge if necessary utilizing a mixed drink stick or tip of a teaspoon. Dry for 10 mins, then pipe inscriptions on top. Leave to dry. Keep the treats in a water/air proof tin for up to 3 days.

HALLOWEEN COOKBOOK

13. Funny Face Tasty Treats

Ingredients

For the treats

- 175g delicate spread
- 100g brilliant caster sugar
- 1 large egg yolk
- ½ tsp vanilla concentrate
- get-up-and-go 1 lemon
- 250g plain flour, in addition to additional for cleaning
- ½ tsp salt

To embellish

- cake pops or lolly sticks
- 200g icing sugar
- 1 large egg white
- pink and brown food shading glues
- pink and gold palatable sparkle (Optional)

Method

1. Beat together the margarine and sugar until pale and velvety, then beat in the yolk, vanilla and pizzazz. Filter the flour and salt into the bowl, then mix into make a

KATYA JOHANSSON

delicate mixture. Part into two level plates, then wrap in stick film and chill for 30 mins, or until firm however not shake hard. In the mean time, warm stove to 180C/160C fan/gas 4. Line two baking sheets with baking material.

2. Flour the work surface, then roll the mixture to 5mm thick. Stamp the mixture with a 8cm round cutter, then re-rolling any trimmings. Utilizing similar cutter, cut a sickle moon and a pointy oval shape from every circle. Pinch the sides of the oval and indent the top and base to make lips. For mustaches, shape the half moon, squeezing a gouge into the highest point of the bend, then change and pinch the closures to make a mustache.

3. Chill for 10 mins, or until firm, then jab cake pop sticks painstakingly into the batter. I discover putting one hand on top of the mixture as I embed the stay with alternate keeps the stick from popping through the surface of the batter.

4. Heat for 12 mins, one plate at once, until pale brilliant. Leave on the plate for 5 mins before lifting to a wire rack (utilize a palette cut as opposed to the sticks) and cooling totally. Make the icing by beating the egg white and the sugar until thick and smooth. Separate into four clusters and shading them two shades of pink and two of brown. Spoon the darker icings into expendable funneling packs and clip off the tips (or utilize a number 2 spout).

5. Pipe mustache and lip diagrams onto the treats. Dry for a couple of mins. Presently relax the paler icings with a couple drops of water until runny. Spoon a little onto every treat and let it surge to the diagram, poking it up to the edge if necessary, utilizing a mixed drink stick or tip of a teaspoon. Dry for 10 mins, then pipe a darker mouth line onto the lips, and crisscrossed lines over the mustaches. Sprinkle with sparkle if utilizing, and leave to set.

Copyright © 2016 – All Rights Reserved | Katya Johansson

HALLOWEEN COOKBOOK

13. Slime Bug Wonderful Cups

Ingredients

- 4 x 135g packs lime jam
- a determination of creature and bug desserts (see tips, beneath, for our choice)
- 2 x 154g packs Oreo bread rolls

Method

1. Make up the jam taking after pack guidelines. Pour 33% of the blend into 12 little glasses or plastic pots. Add two or three bugs to every pot, then leave to set in the refrigerator, continuing outstanding jam at room temperature.
2. When set, add more bugs to every container (incline some against edges, so they stand out the top). Pour over 33% of the jam and leave to set in the ice chest. Rehash with residual bugs and jam.
3. For the dirt garnish, put treats in a plastic pack and, utilizing a moving pin, bash into morsels, then tip onto a plate.
4. Just before serving, sprinkle a layer of soil over every set jam, then top with a mushroom, a slug and a few ants or your decision of dreadful little animals.

Copyright © 2016 – All Rights Reserved | Katya Johansson

14. Sausage Mummy Delicious scoops

Ingredients

- oil, for lubing
- 1 tbsp Honey
- 1 tbsp ketchup
- 2 tsp French's yellow mustard
- 12 chipolata
- container of 6 good to go croissant (look in the chiller cupboards close to the cake in the general stores)

Method

1. Warm stove to 200C/180C fan/gas 6 and brush 2 baking plate with a little oil. Blend the Honey, ketchup and mustard together in a bowl, then brush over the chipolata hotdogs.
2. Unroll the croissant batter and separation into 3 rectangles. Pinch together the slanting punctured creases, then cut into long thin strips – you ought to get around 16 for every rectangle.
3. Wind the little croissant strips around the chipolatas, leaving a little hole toward one side to make an opening for the eyes. Put on baking plate and prepare for 20 mins. Cool somewhat, then, utilizing the mustard, speck a couple of minimal yellow eyes on to every mummy.

HALLOWEEN COOKBOOK

Serve warm with gleam oblivious goo (see runs well with, beneath) and/or your most loved plunge.

KATYA JOHANSSON

15. Best Witch's Cauldron

Ingredients

- 1 vast round roll of bread
- 1 egg
- 100g pack poppy seed
- 1kg butternut squash lumps
- 1 onion
- 2 garlic clove, peeled
- 400g can cream of tomato soup
- 1 tsp ground cumin
- 1 tsp ground coriander
- 2 tbsp bean stew sauce, we utilized Lingham's
- additional toasted pitta bread, Sausage mummies (see runs well with) and cucumber sticks, to plunge

Method

1. Cut the finish off the piece, then scoop out the delicate bread from the center of the base, leaving the hull around 2.5cm thick the distance round. Cut the bread out in pieces for toasting to serve, or basically get the children to haul it out with their fingers.
2. Warm stove to 200C/180C fan/gas 6. Brush the outside of the large "cauldron" and top done with beaten egg, then roll the hull of the cauldron and cover in poppy seeds to coat – tipping them onto a major supper plate first makes this less demanding. Sit on baking sheets,

HALLOWEEN COOKBOOK

poppy seed-sides up, and prepare for 10 mins. Put aside until you are prepared to party.

3. Bring a huge dish of salted water to the boil, include the butternut squash, onion and garlic, then stew until the squash and onion are delicate. Drain truly well, then tip into a food processor or blender with the soup, flavors, bean stew sauce and some flavoring and whizz to a smooth purée (or set back in the pot and whizz with a stick-blender). Put aside.

4. Just before the visitors are because of arrive, warmth the plunge in a microwave or pan – it ought to be decent and hot. Spoon into the bread cauldron, pop on the cover and convey to the gathering table, prepared for dunking in the Sausage mummies (see runs well with), cucumber sticks and more toasted bread. Also, as the plunge vanishes, you can begin to eat the cauldron, as well!

Copyright © 2016 – All Rights Reserved | Katya Johansson

KATYA JOHANSSON

16. Dracula's Tasty Punch

Ingredients

- 2l cherry juice
- peel from 3 oranges
- 1 thumb-sized red stew, penetrated a couple times however left entirety
- 3 cinnamon sticks
- 10 clove
- 6 cuts ginger

Method

1. Tip the cherry juice, orange peel, bean stew, cinnamon sticks, cloves and ginger into a substantial pan. Stew for 5 mins, then kill the warmth. Leave to cool, then chill for no less than 4 hrs. or up to 2 days – the more you abandon it the more serious the flavors. On the off chance that serving to youthful kids, take the bean stew out following a couple of hours.
2. When you're prepared to serve, empty the juice into a container. Serve in glass containers or glasses and pop a straw in each. Dangle a teeth sweet from every glass.

Copyright © 2016 – All Rights Reserved | Katya Johansson

HALLOWEEN COOKBOOK

17. Eerie eyeball pops

Ingredients

- 100g/4oz Madeira cake
- 100g Oreo treat
- 100g bar milk chocolate, dissolved
- 200g bar white chocolate, dissolved
- 10 wooden stick
- ½ little pumpkin
- on the other hand butternut squash, deseeded, to stand pops in

Method

1. Break the Madeira cake and treats into the bowl of a food processor, pour in the liquefied milk chocolate and whizz to consolidate.
2. Tip the blend into a bowl, then utilize your hands to move into around 10 walnut-sized balls. Chill for 2 hrs. until truly firm.
3. Push a stick into every ball, then precisely spoon the white chocolate over the cake balls to totally cover. Stand the cake pops in the pumpkin, then press a Smartie onto the surface while wet. Chill again until the chocolate has set. Before serving, utilizing the icing pens, add an understudy to each Smartie and wiggly red veins to the eyeballs.

Copyright © 2016 – All Rights Reserved | Katya Johansson

KATYA JOHANSSON

18. Tasty Halloween jam

Ingredients

- 2 x 135g packs strawberry or raspberry jam
- 425g can lychee in syrup
- 12-14 little seedless green grapes
- 12-14 dull shaded jam beans
- 80g white marzipan
- 6-8 entire whitened almonds
- red channeling gel or red icing in a tube

Method

1. Cut the jam into 3D squares with scissors and place in a bowl. Include 400ml boiling water and mix ceaselessly until broke down.
2. Drain the lychees, saving the juice. Put the juice in a measuring container and make up to 400ml with chilly water. Add to the disintegrated jam.
3. Pour around a fourth of the jam into a reasonable glass dish and place in the refrigerator to set.
4. Take a grape and delicately push a jam bean into the middle, utilizing the opening where the stalk has been. At that point delicately push the grape into a lychee. Rehash with the rest of the grapes and lychees to make eyeballs.
5. To make the spooky fingers, isolate the marzipan into 6 and shape into hotdogs the extent of a finger. Pipe somewhat red gel toward one side and connect an

Copyright © 2016 – All Rights Reserved | Katya Johansson

HALLOWEEN COOKBOOK

almond to speak to a fingernail. Utilizing a little blade stamp three or four lines mostly down the finger to make a knuckle.

6. At the point when the jam is set, orchestrate a large portion of the eyeballs over the surface, add more jam and come back to the cooler.
7. At the point when this has set, organize the rest of the eyeballs over the jam. Put the spooky fingers against the side of the bowl. Pour over the rest of the jam and place in the refrigerator to set. Serve in the bowl.

19. Healthy Orange Pumpkin Treats

Ingredients

- 140g margarine
- 175g plain flour
- 50g icing sugar
- finely ground pizzazz 1 medium orange

For the filling

- 100g mascarpone
- 1 tsp icing sugar
- 25g plain chocolate (55% cocoa solids is fine), liquefied

For the coating

- 50g icing sugar
- around 1 tbsp squeezed orange

Method

1. Preheat the broiler to fan 160C/routine 180C/gas 4. Put the margarine in a bowl and beat with a wooden spoon until smooth. Include the flour, icing sugar and orange

HALLOWEEN COOKBOOK

get-up-and-go and beat together to make a softest mixture. Massage into a ball and wrap in stick film. Chill for 60 minutes.

2. Roll the batter out on a delicately floured surface to a thickness of around 3mm. Cut 24 hovers with a 7.5 cm round plain cutter. Put them on two or three baking sheets.
3. Utilizing a little sharp blade, cut out Hallowe'en confronts on 12 of the circles. Get together the extra roll batter and press into pumpkin stem shapes, trimming with a sharp blade. Press to the highest point of every bread with a blade to join. Make lines on the face scones with the back of a round bladed blade, to resemble the markings on a pumpkin. Prepare every one of the bread rolls for around 15 minutes until pale brilliant. Leave to set for some time, then cool totally on a wire rack.
4. Blend the coating Ingredients to make a smooth, runny icing, including more squeeze if necessary, then put aside. For the filling, beat the mascarpone with the icing sugar, then mix in the cooled liquefied chocolate.
5. Spread the filling over the cooled plain bread rolls, then press the "face" ones on top – do this fair before you need to eat them, else they go delicate. Brush with the coating, utilizing a perfect paint brush or baked good brush. Eat that day.

20. Haunted Cemetery Cake

Ingredients

To Garnish

- 1 egg white
- 50g icing sugar
- 200ml single cream
- 200g dull chocolate, finely cleaved
- 125g rich tea finger rolls
- 100g twofold chocolate treats
- 25g white chocolate
- silver balls, to adorn

For the cake

- 85g cocoa powder
- 200g flour
- 375g light brown muscovado sugar
- 4 eggs
- 200ml milk
- 175ml vegetable oil

Method

HALLOWEEN COOKBOOK

1. To make the phantoms, warm broiler to 110C/90C fan/gas ¼. Whip the egg white in a perfect bowl until hardened pinnacles shape. Speed in the sugar a tbsp at once and continue racing for two or three mins until the blend is thick and takes after shaving froth. Tenderly spoon the blend into a vast cooler sack, then cut a 1.5cm gap in one of the corners. Cover a baking sheet with some baking material. Deliberately squeeze a little hover of whipped egg white out of the pack, pulling upwards as you do to make a phantom shape. Rehash until the blend is spent – you ought to get around 15 apparitions. Heat for 1½ hrs. until fresh. Can be put away in a water/air proof container for up to 2 days.
2. Presently make the cake. Warm stove to 180C/160C fan/gas 4. Tip the cocoa powder, flour and sugar into a vast bowl, separating any bunches of sugar. Combine the eggs, milk and oil in a measuring cup or bowl, then pour over the dry Ingredients and blend everything together until smooth. Oil and line a profound baking dish (20 x 30 x 5cm) with baking material. Pour in the cake blend and heat for 30 mins. Leave to cool, then turn out onto a serving plate. On the other hand, wrap well and store for up to 2 days.
3. Wrap up the cake: warm cream in a pan until simply boiling. Put the dim chocolate in a vast bowl and pour over the hot cream. Blend until the chocolate softens. Utilize a spotless brush to paint a layer of chocolate more than 7 rich tea finger scones, then put aside to cool. Pour whatever is left of the chocolate blend over the cake and cover up with a blade. Whizz the chocolate treats, or bash in a cooler pack with a moving pin, until little morsels frame. Sprinkle over the highest point of the cake.
4. Put the white chocolate in a little bowl, set over a container of stewing water. Leave for 5 mins or until

-39-

Copyright © 2016 – All Rights Reserved | Katya Johansson

KATYA JOHANSSON

softened, then spoon into a little cooler pack. Sit tight for 10 mins so the blend is not very runny, then cut a little gap in one corner of the pack. Pipe out 2 little blobs onto every apparition, put a silver ball on each to make eyes, then pipe out reasonable words and shapes on the tombstones. Leave for 30 mins to set, then push the bread tombstones into the cake and mastermind the apparitions around. To get the apparitions to 'fly', push a thin wire (you can get these from a flower vendor shop – recollect to evacuate before eating) into the base of the phantom, then place in the cake, concealing the wire behind a headstone.

21. Chocolate Creepy Crawly Treats

Ingredients

- 200g dim or milk chocolate, broken into pieces
- 113g pack liquorice Catherine wheels (we utilized Barratts)
- 2 x 154g packs Oreo treats
- white and dark icing pens

Method

1. Soften the chocolate in a heatproof bowl over a dish of scarcely stewing water. Once softened, kill the warmth and leave the chocolate in the bowl to keep warm while you collect the creepy crawlies.
2. Unroll a portion of the liquorice haggles into 2-3cm lengths to use as the Chocolate creepy crawlies' legs.
3. Splodge a little tsp of chocolate onto half of the treats. Organize eight liquorice legs on top, then sandwich with another treat. Spread some more chocolate on top of the second treat to cover, then put some place cool to set.
4. Utilize the icing pens to include eyes, by first blobbing two major dabs of white what tops off an already good thing, with two littler dabs of dark icing.

22. Tasty Eyeball pasta

Ingredients

- 100g cherry tomato
- 150g pack scaled down mozzarella balls, drained
- modest bunch basil
- 400g green tagliatelle
- 350g jug tomato sauce
- 4 tbsp crisp pesto

Method

1. Divide the cherry tomatoes and utilize a little, sharp blade or a teaspoon to evacuate the seeds. Sliced the mozzarella balls down the middle. Put one half inside every tomato, trimming the edges if important to fit it in. Either cut the littlest circles you can from a basil leaf or finely slash the leaves and scrunch into little circles. Put one at the focal point of every mozzarella ball.
2. Boil the pasta. In the interim, warm through the tomato sauce. At the point when the tagliatelle is cooked, drain and mix through the pesto and any outstanding basil, cleaved finely. Partition between 4-6 serving bowls. Spoon over some tomato sauce, then organize the stuffed tomato eyeballs on top.

HALLOWEEN COOKBOOK

23. Delicious Spider Chocolate Biscuits

Ingredients

- 50g dim chocolate (55% cocoa solids is fine)
- 85g margarine
- 1 tbsp milk
- water or coffee
- 200g flour
- ½ tsp bicarbonate of pop
- 85g light muscovado sugar
- 50g brilliant caster sugar
- 1 egg
- 142ml container soured cream
- 100g dull chocolate (as above)
- 100g white chocolate

Method

1. Preheat the stove to fan 170C/traditional 190C/gas 5 and line a biscuit tin with 10 paper biscuit cases. Break the chocolate into a heatproof bowl, include the margarine and fluid. Liquefy in the microwave on Medium for 30-45 seconds (or set the bowl over a container of delicately stewing water). Blend and leave the blend to cool.
2. Blend the flour, bicarbonate of pop and both sugars in a bowl. Beat the egg in another bowl and blend in the

KATYA JOHANSSON

soured cream, then pour this on the flour blend and include the cooled chocolate. Mix just to consolidate – don't overmix or it will get intense.

3. Spoon the blend into the cases to around seventy five percent full. Heat for 20 minutes until well risen. Relax the edges with a round-bladed blade, let them sit in the tins for a couple of minutes, then lift out and cool on a wire rack.
4. For the garnish, make two channeling packs out of greaseproof paper (or cut the closures off two clean plastic sacks). Break the dull and white chocolate into particular bowls and dissolve in the microwave on Medium for 2 minutes (or over a dish as in step 1). Put 2 spoonful of dull chocolate in one sack and the same of white chocolate in the other.
5. Working with one muffin at once, spread with dim chocolate from the bowl, giving it a chance to rundown somewhat, then pipe four concentric circles of white chocolate on top. Utilizing a little stick, drag through the circles at general interims, from the middle to the edge, to make a spider web impact. Rehash with four more muffins. On the staying five, spread over the white chocolate and enliven with the dim. Best eaten the day they're made – stunningly better while the chocolate's delicate.

24. Chocolate Arachnid Tasty Jams

Ingredients

- 1l smooth squeezed orange
- 6 strips gelatin
- 25g dull chocolate

Method

1. Warm the squeezed orange in a medium-estimate container until almost boiling. Cover the gelatin with chilly water and leave for 5 mins until light and relaxed. Squeeze out any abundance water. Take the container off the warmth and blend in the gelatin until disintegrated. Give the blend a chance to cool somewhat, then partition between 10 serving dishes. Put in the ice chest for no less than 5 hrs. or ideally overnight.
2. Cover a baking sheet with some baking material. Soften the chocolate either in the microwave (1-2 mins ought to do it) or in a bowl set over a little skillet of boiling water. Empty the softened chocolate into a little cooler pack. Make a funneling pack by clipping off a small bit of one corner. Presently pipe out 10 cobweb shapes onto the baking material: pipe a hover with a littler hover inside, then pipe lines turning out from the middle like the spokes of a wheel. Put the chocolate bug catching networks in the ice chest to solidify. Just before serving,

KATYA JOHANSSON

precisely peel away every bug catching network from the material and place on top of a jam.

25. Pumpkin Witch Delicious Cupcakes

Ingredients

- 1 c. cocoa powder
- 1 c. universally handy flour
- ¾ tsp. baking pop
- ¾ tsp. fine ocean salt
- ½ tsp. ground cinnamon
- ½ tsp. ground ginger
- 13 tsp. ground allspice
- 1 c. brown sugar
- 11 tbsp. unsalted margarine
- 3 large eggs
- ¾ c. pumpkin puree
- 1 tsp. vanilla concentrate
- Hazelnut Cream Cheese Frosting
- 6 oz. dark treat softens
- 12 pointy sugar frozen custards
- Dark paper cupcake liners
- Hazelnut Cream Cheese Frosting
- 1 bundle cream cheddar
- 2 stick unsalted margarine
- 1 c. confectioners' sugar
- ¼ c. hazelnut chocolate cream spread
- 1 tsp. vanilla

KATYA JOHANSSON

METHOD

1. Warm stove to 350 degrees F.
2. Whisk initial 7 Ingredients in a medium bowl to join. In a large bowl, beat sugar and margarine utilizing an electric blender until light and cushy. Include eggs and pumpkin puree, and beat to consolidate. Mix in vanilla. Include flour blend, and beat until all around joined.
3. Line a 12-cup muffin container with paper liners. Separate blend among arranged muffin cups, filling every 3/4 full.
4. Heat for 20 to 25 minutes or until a toothpick embedded in the focal point of a cupcake tells the truth.
5. Line a baking sheet with material paper. Microwave sweet melts in a warmth evidence bowl on high for 30 seconds, mixing at 10 second interims. Utilize a cake brush to cover the frozen treats with the sweet dissolve. Set on baking sheet to dry. Cut a 1 3/4 crawl measurement opening in the focal point of a paper cupcake liner. Put over sweetened up frozen treat to frame the overflow of the witch's cap.
6. Ice cupcakes with Hazelnut Cream Cheese Frosting. Beat each with a witch's cap.
7. To make the Hazelnut Cream Cheese Frosting: Place all Ingredients in a large bowl. Beat until light and soft utilizing the whisk connection of an electric blender.

HALLOWEEN COOKBOOK

26. Amazing Mummy Hot Dogs

Ingredients

- 4 large eggs
- 3/4 cup water, warmed to 100 to 110 degrees F
- 3 tablespoons sugar
- Two .25-ounce bundles dynamic dry yeast
- 1 stick (4 ounces) unsalted margarine, at room temperature, in addition to additional for lubing the bowl
- 4 cups generally useful flour, in addition to additional for tidying
- 1 teaspoon genuine salt
- 3 bundles all-meat franks or veggie canines (24 to 36 wieners)
- 1/4 cup entire dark olives
- 1/2 cup mayonnaise
- Serving proposals: ketchup and mustard

Method

1. Preheat the broiler to 400 degrees F.
2. In a little bowl, whisk together 2 of the eggs and 1 tablespoon dilute until the whites break and the blend is thin and runny. Put the egg wash aside for later utilize.
3. In a medium bowl, whisk together the 3/4 cup warm water, sugar and yeast until broke up and bubbly. Utilizing a wooden spoon, include the spread, 2 cups of

KATYA JOHANSSON

the flour and the rest of the 2 eggs and blend until a mixture begins to shape. Put the batter in the bowl of a stand blender fitted with the mixture snare and blend on low speed. Blend the salt into the rest of the 2 cups flour and continuously add the flour to the batter with the blender still on low speed. Keep on mixing until the batter is smooth, 3 to 5 minutes. Put the batter in a daintily lubed bowl to rest at room temperature until it pairs in size, 1 to 2 hours.

4. Punch down the mixture and gap it into equal parts. On a gently floured work surface, take off 1 parcel of the mixture to around 1/4 crawl thick with a moving pin or dowel. Cut the batter into 1/4-to 1/2-creep wide strips, utilizing a blade or pizza wheel. Reveal the rest of the batter and rehash.
5. Wrap the wieners with the pieces of mixture beginning toward one side and wrapping to the next end, leaving a little space for the eyes, covering the strips if fancied.
6. Put the wrapped wieners on a material lined baking sheet around 2 creeps separated and brush with the held egg wash. Heat until brilliant brown, 12 to 17 minutes.
7. Cut the olives into quarters from end to end utilizing a little paring blade. Expel a portion of the inside meat from the olives utilizing similar blade. Utilizing the little end of a little funneling tip, punch out the eyes for the wieners.
8. Put the mayonnaise in a little funneling pack. At the point when the mutts cool marginally, pipe the mayonnaise into 2 little circles associated in the inside. Put the olive pieces in the mayonnaise to make the completed eyes. Rehash for the staying sausage. Serve the mummy franks warm with ketchup and mustard.

HALLOWEEN COOKBOOK

27. Amazing Deviled Eggs

Ingredients

- 9 hard-boiled eggs
- 3/4 cup mayonnaise
- 2 teaspoons Dijon mustard
- 1/8 teaspoon salt
- Dash ground dark pepper
- 1 teaspoon orange gel shading
- 1/2 teaspoon dark gel shading
- 2 green onions, green part as it were

Method

1. Sliced the eggs down the middle the long way and evacuate the yolks to a medium bowl. Delicately wash the egg whites and pat dry with a perfect fabric or paper towel. Lay the eggs level on a paper-towel-lined baking sheet so they don't move around when filling.
2. Squash the yolks until smooth. Add 2 to 4 tablespoons of the mayonnaise and the mustard. Include the salt and pepper and blend until joined. Blend in the orange shading to make the filling splendid orange, similar to the shade of a pumpkin. Put the blend into a channeling sack for filling the eggs.
3. In a different little bowl, blend the rest of the 8 to 10 tablespoons mayonnaise and the dark shading until dim dark. Put the mayonnaise in a little funneling pack fitted with a little (number 2) tip.

4. Utilizing a little blade, cut the green onions into 1/2-crawl pieces for the stems of the jack-o-lamps, and after that place in a little bowl.
5. Pipe the orange filling into every egg half, making a round hill in the middle to make the pumpkin. Pipe the dark mayonnaise onto the filling: make two little triangles for the eyes and a crisscross line for the mouth. Put a bit of green onion at the highest point of the filling by the eyes to make the stem of the jack-o-lamp. Serve instantly or hold for up to 2 hours.

28. Healthy Pumpkin Cake

Ingredients

Cake:

- 2 1/4 cups generally useful flour, in addition to additional for the dishes
- 1 cup vegetable oil
- 1 cup granulated sugar
- 1 cup all around pressed brown sugar
- 3 substantial eggs
- One 14-ounce can pumpkin puree
- 3/4 cup acrid cream
- 1/2 teaspoons vanilla concentrate
- 1/2 teaspoons baking pop
- 1 teaspoon salt
- 1 teaspoon crisply ground nutmeg
- 1/2 teaspoon ground ginger
- 1/4 teaspoon allspice
- 1 teaspoon salt

Buttercream:

- 1/2 cups granulated sugar
- 3/4 cup vast egg whites
- 4 1/2 sticks (1/8 pounds) unsalted margarine, at room temperature

KATYA JOHANSSON

- 2 teaspoons vanilla concentrate
- Pinch salt
- Gel or glue food shading, for buttercream and marzipan
- 4 ounces marzipan

METHOD

1. Preheat the broiler to 350 degrees F.
2. For the cake: Butter and flour the stainless steel bowls. In a stand blender fitted with the oar connection, join the oil, granulated sugar, brown sugar and eggs. When they are very much consolidated include the pumpkin puree, sharp cream and vanilla. In a different bowl, whisk together the flour, baking pop, nutmeg, ginger, allspice and salt. Add the dry Ingredients to the pumpkin blend and combine until everything arrives in a smooth hitter.
3. Isolate the player among the four arranged bowls and place them on baking sheets. Prepare until a toothpick confesses all, around 40 to 50 minutes (this may rely on upon the state of your dishes). It is alright on the off chance that they don't prepare totally level, odds are they won't.
4. Turn the cakes out onto a baking sheet and permit them to cool totally. They can be made ahead and refrigerated for up to 2 days or solidified for 2 weeks.

FOR THE BUTTERCREAM:

1. In the bowl of your stand blender, join the sugar and egg whites. The blend will be thick and grainy. Put the bowl over a twofold boiler and blend with an elastic spatula until the sugar is totally softened. This can take a few

HALLOWEEN COOKBOOK

minutes. You need to brush the sides down with the spatula to ensure all the sugar is liquefied and no grains are sticking to the sides. Feel the egg blend between your fingers to check for graininess. When it is totally smooth and has no grains left, put it on your stand blender and beat with the whip connection on medium fast. Beat it until it is light, feathery, and shiny and the bowl feels pretty much room temperature. (In the event that the whites are not chilled adequately it will dissolve the margarine when you include it.)

2. Once the egg whites are whipped and cooled, include the margarine, 2 tablespoons at once, on medium speed. Cautioning: After you have included about portion of the spread, the blend may look coagulated and runny. This is typical and you ought to keep including whatever remains of the margarine. When you have wrapped up the spread and it has blended on medium speed for around a moment, the buttercream ought to be rich and gleaming looking once more. Include the vanilla and salt. Utilize food shading to accomplish the shading orange you like.
3. Gather the cake: Spread a thin layer of buttercream over the level side of every cake. Sandwich 2 of the cakes together to make a circle.
4. Spread a thick layer of icing over the whole cake, leaving only the exceptionally base free of icing. Utilize a spatula to make the stripes at the edges of the pumpkin, and after that level out the top just somewhat.
5. Refirgerate the pumpkin cake to set the buttercream, no less than 60 minutes. Rehash with the other two half adjusts to make a second cake.
6. While the cakes are chilling, shading the marzipan with green food shading. (Utilize gloves to keep your hands clean.) Sculpt stems and the wavy rings from the green marzipan. Permit them to sit out at room temperature

for a couple of hours or overnight so they will hold their shape.
7. Set the chilled cakes on stands and beautify with the stems and wavy rings. Serve at room temperature. It is alright to leave the embellished cake at room temperature for up to 24 hours.

29. Amazing Pumpkin Cookies

INGREDIENTS

- 2 1/2 cups universally handy flour
- 1 teaspoon baking powder
- 1 teaspoon baking pop
- 2 teaspoons ground cinnamon
- 1/2 teaspoon ground nutmeg
- 1/2 teaspoon ground cloves
- 1/2 teaspoon salt
- 1/2 cup margarine, mollified
- 1/2 cups white sugar
- 1 cup canned pumpkin puree
- 1 egg
- 1 teaspoon vanilla concentrate
- 2 cups confectioners' sugar
- 3 tablespoons milk
- 1 tablespoon liquefied spread
- 1 teaspoon vanilla concentrate

METHOD

1. Preheat stove to 350 degrees F (175 degrees C). Consolidate flour, baking powder, baking pop, cinnamon, nutmeg, ground cloves, and salt; put aside.
2. In a medium bowl, cream together the 1/2 cup of spread and white sugar. Include pumpkin, egg, and 1 teaspoon vanilla to spread blend, and beat until smooth. Blend in

KATYA JOHANSSON

dry Ingredients. Drop on treat sheet by tablespoonful; level somewhat.

3. Heat for 15 to 20 minutes in the preheated broiler. Cool treats, then shower coat with fork.
4. To Make Glaze: Combine confectioners' sugar, milk, 1 tablespoon softened margarine, and 1 teaspoon vanilla. Include milk as required, to accomplish showering consistency.

30. Amazing Goblin Flatbreads

Ingredients

- Pizza batter, locally acquired or custom made
- additional virgin olive oil
- Salt

Method

1. Preheat stove to 475 degrees. Take off batter, and utilize a paring blade, scissors, or treat cutters to make highlights (we utilized sickle, football, and jewel shapes).
2. Brush with oil, and sprinkle with salt. Prepare until "demon lair," 10 to 12 minutes.

31. Amazing Halloween Ghosties

Ingredients

- 1 (12 ounce) bundle white chocolate chips, or as required
- 24 nut formed nutty spread sandwich treats
- 48 scaled down chocolate chips

Method

1. Put chocolate chips into a microwave-safe bowl and warmth on low in microwave for 1 minute; blend. Keep heating on low a few more times, 30 seconds on end, mixing after every time, until white chocolate is warm and smooth.
2. Utilize 2 forks to plunge treats into white chocolate; set treats on sheets of waxed paper. Put 2 small scale chocolate chips onto one end of every treat for eyes; put treats aside until covering has solidified, around 20 minutes.

32. Amazing Cauldron Curry

Ingredients

For the Curry Paste (Makes One Cup)

- 1 tablespoon entire coriander seeds, toasted
- 2 teaspoons entire cumin seeds, toasted
- 1 teaspoon entire dark peppercorns, toasted
- 1 teaspoon coarse salt
- 3 serrano chilies, cut
- 1/2 cup crisp cilantro
- 2 stalks crisp lemongrass, trimmed and slashed (1/2 cup)
- 8 garlic cloves, minced (1/4 cup)
- 2 scallions, slashed (1/4 cup)
- 2 tablespoons hacked peeled new ginger
- 2 tablespoons new lime juice
- 1 tablespoon finely ground lime get-up-and-go (from 2 limes)

For the Stew

- 2 ounces spinach (1 cup)
- 1 can (14 ounces) unsweetened normal coconut milk
- 1 can (14 ounces) unsweetened light coconut milk
- 1 medium zucchini, quartered longwise and cut 1 creep thick (2 1/4 cups)

KATYA JOHANSSON

- 12 ounces boneless, skinless chicken bosoms, cut into 1-creep pieces
- 12 ounces boneless, skinless chicken thighs, cut into 1-creep pieces
- Coarse salt and crisply ground pepper
- 3/4 cup crisp basil
- Serrano chilies, meagerly cut, for topping
- Nauseous Squash with Rice
- Lime wedges, for serving

METHOD

1. Make the curry glue: Grind coriander, cumin, peppercorns, and salt with a mortar and pestle, or with the base of a heavy skillet. Include remaining Ingredients, and crush until a glue frames. (Curry glue can be refrigerated for up to 2 weeks or solidified for up to 3 months.)
2. Make the stew: Puree 5 tablespoons curry glue, the spinach, and 1 cup consistent coconut milk in a blender until smooth. Save remaining curry glue for another utilization.
3. Bring staying normal coconut milk and the light coconut milk to a boil in a medium Dutch stove or heavy stockpot. Lessen warm, blend in curry-spinach blend, and stew for 5 minutes. Include zucchini, and cook until somewhat delicate, around 5 minutes. Include chicken, and season with salt and pepper. Cook until zucchini is delicate and chicken is cooked through, around 5 minutes. Include basil, and topping with serrano chilies. Present with rice and lime wedges.

33. Monster Fingers with Cheese Paws

Ingredients

- Pimento Cheese
- 2 cups horse feed grows

Method

1. Put four 3/4 cup hills of pimento cheddar on a cutting board or serving platter. Stick five women's fingers or men's toes into every hill to make a paw.
2. Best every paw with 1/2 cup hay grows. Present with residual fingers and toes.

34. Amazing Guacamole with Black Beans

Ingredients

- 1 can (15 1/2 ounces) dark beans, drained and flushed
- 1/2 teaspoons coarse salt
- 1/2 large white onion, finely cleaved
- 1 teaspoon minced jalapeno chili (seeds evacuated, if craved)
- 1/2 teaspoons minced chipotle in adobo
- 1 little clove garlic, minced
- 2 tablespoons in addition to 1 teaspoon crisp lime juice (from 1 to 2 limes)
- 2 ready avocados, hollowed and peeled
- 1/4 cup hacked cilantro
- Blue corn tortilla chips, for serving

Method

1. Consolidate beans, salt, onion, jalapeno, chipotle, garlic, and lime squeeze in a bowl. Crush avocados; blend into bean blend with cilantro. Serve quickly, with chips.

35. Wonderful Monster Mucus

Ingredients

- 2 dozen clams, shucked, juices held
- Great Cocktail Sauce

Method

1. Put clams and their juices in a tall glass; present with mixed drink sauce.

KATYA JOHANSSON

36. Healthy Spinach Ricotta Skulls

Ingredients

- 1 container (15 ounces) part-skim ricotta cheddar
- Olive-oil, cooking spray
- 1 bundle crisp spinach (or a 10-ounce sack), stems evacuated, washed well and dried
- 1/2 cups inexactly pressed new basil leaves (from 1 group)
- 1/4 teaspoon crisp ground nutmeg
- Coarse salt and crisp ground pepper
- 2 vast entire eggs, in addition to 1 egg white
- Saltines, for serving

Method

2. Wrap ricotta firmly in cheesecloth; put in a colander over a huge bowl. Put a heavy question, (for example, a bowl or canned great) on top; let drain in the icebox no less than 3 hours (or up to overnight).
3. Preheat stove to 350 degrees. Coat a 10-crawl container with cooking spray. In a food processor, consolidate drained ricotta, spinach, basil, nutmeg, 1 teaspoon salt, and 1/4 teaspoon pepper. Handle until smooth, around 1 minute, scratching sides of bowl as required. Include entire eggs and egg white; handle for 5 seconds. Empty blend into arranged dish; heat until set and simply

Copyright © 2016 – All Rights Reserved | Katya Johansson

HALLOWEEN COOKBOOK

brown around the edges, 30 to 35 minutes. Let cool totally on a wire rack, then refrigerate, covered, until chilly, ideally overnight. To unmold, run a paring blade around edge before expelling side of container.

4. Cut into quarters. Utilizing a wide spatula, exchange to a cutting board covered with cooking spray. Removed shapes with a skull-formed treat cutter covered with spray (if cutter doesn't accompany eyes and a mouth, utilize aspic cutters to make highlights). Utilizing a cotton swab, tenderly squeeze skulls out specifically onto saltines (leave eye and nose shapes in cutter).

Copyright © 2016 – All Rights Reserved | Katya Johansson

37. Amazing Spiderweb Eggs

Ingredients

- 1 dozen huge eggs
- 8 cups water
- 2 cups solidified blueberries
- Dim ocean salt, for serving
- Newly ground dark pepper, for serving

Method

1. Put eggs in single layer in a huge pot, and cover with water and blueberries. Heat to the point of boiling. Expel from warmth. Cover; let stand 10 minutes.
2. Utilizing a spoon, expel eggs each one in turn, and place on a collapsed kitchen towel. Softly break shell on agree with the handle of a whisk or a wooden spoon. Exchange egg to medium bowl; cover with cooking water. Rehash with outstanding eggs. Give eggs a chance to cool totally in water in fridge.
3. Painstakingly peel shells from eggs. Present with salt and pepper.

HALLOWEEN COOKBOOK

38. Halloween Peas

Ingredients

- 4 cuts white sandwich bread
- 1/4 cup additional virgin olive oil
- Coarse salt and crisply ground pepper
- 4 tablespoons unsalted spread
- 1 onion, cut into 1/2-creep pieces
- 1/4 cup generally useful flour
- 2 1/2 cups milk
- 1/2 cup heavy cream
- 1/2 teaspoon newly ground nutmeg
- Pinch of cayenne pepper
- 2 boxes (10 ounces each) solidified peas defrosted and drained well

Method

1. Preheat stove to 350 degrees. Utilizing format and a paring blade, cut bread into shapes. (On the other hand, cut bread freehand.) Place on a baking sheet; brush bread shapes with oil. Season with salt and pepper. Toast in broiler until brilliant, 10 to 12 minutes.
2. Warm margarine in a substantial pan over medium warmth until frothing. Include onion; cook, mixing once in a while, until delicate, around 4 minutes. Mix in flour; cook, blending continually, until blend starts to turn brilliant, around 4 minutes.

Copyright © 2016 – All Rights Reserved | Katya Johansson

KATYA JOHANSSON

3. Whisking continually, slowly include milk. Cook until blend thickens, 3 to 5 minutes. Blend in cream, nutmeg, and cayenne. Season with salt and pepper. Blend in peas; cook until warmed through, around 3 minutes.
4. Exchange pea blend to a shallow serving dish. Orchestrate gravestone bread garnishes on top.

39. Wonderful Cured Epidermis

Ingredients

- 24 1/8-creep thick cuts prosciutto

Method

1. Preheat stove to 400 degrees. Line a baking sheet with paper towels; put aside.
2. Line baking sheet with a nonstick baking mat; lay prosciutto cuts level in an even layer on baking sheet. Exchange to stove and prepare until fresh, around 15 minutes. Exchange to a wire rack set over baking sheet fixed with paper towel to drain off fat; serve.

40. Wonderful Bat Wings

Ingredients

- 1 cup soy sauce
- 1/4 cup in addition to 2 tablespoons clam sauce
- 1/4 cup light-brown sugar
- 1/4 cup dark bean sauce
- 1 teaspoon dark glue food shading
- 20 large entire chicken wings with tips

Method

1. In a medium bowl, whisk together soy sauce, clam sauce, sugar, dark bean sauce, and food shading. Set 1/3 cup soy sauce blend aside.
2. Put chicken wings in an large plastic pack and pour remaining soy sauce blend over wings; seal sack. Turn sack until wings are very much covered. Refrigerate, and let marinate for no less than 2 hours and up to overnight, turning chicken wings at regular intervals to coat.
3. Preheat broiler to 375 degrees. Line 2 baking sheets with material paper or a nonstick baking mat; put aside.
4. Expel wings from marinade, shaking off any abundance; dispose of marinade. Put them in an even layer on arranged baking sheets, orchestrating them so wings are expanded. Prepare until juices run clear, 20 to 25 minutes, brushing with saved soy sauce blend like clockwork. Expel from stove and brush with any residual

HALLOWEEN COOKBOOK

soy sauce blend. Let cool somewhat on a wire rack before serving.

KATYA JOHANSSON

3. Bring down broiler to 325 degrees. In a food processor, beat almonds, broiled red peppers, pimenton, mint, vinegar, garlic, and 3/4 teaspoon salt to a coarse glue, around 1 minute. With machine running, include 1 tablespoon oil in a moderate, constant flow through the tube until smooth. Exchange to a bowl.
4. Put potatoes on a rimmed baking sheet and hurl with residual 1/2 teaspoons oil and 1/4 teaspoon salt. Broil in stove (without moving potatoes on the dish) until skins are somewhat fresh and potatoes are delicate, around 1/2 hours. Serve potatoes warm or at room temperature, with sauce as an afterthought.

HALLOWEEN COOKBOOK

43. FRENCH ONION SOUPS

INGREDIENTS

- 3 tablespoons olive oil
- 2 pounds yellow onions, daintily cut
- Coarse salt and new ground pepper
- 1/2 cup white wine
- 8 cups hand crafted or low-sodium chicken stock
- 4 sprigs thyme
- 3 tablespoons port (Optional)
- 1/2 baguette, cut 1/4 creep thick and toasted
- 12 ounces Morbier cheddar, cut into 4-to 5-creep long pieces

METHOD

1. In a large pot or Dutch stove with a tight-fitting top, warm oil over medium. Include onions and cook, mixing infrequently, until dull brilliant and caramelized, 30 to 40 minutes. Season with salt and pepper. Include wine, and heat to the point of boiling over medium-high warmth; keep boiling until lessened considerably.
2. Include stock and thyme. Heat to the point of boiling; diminish warmth and stew until onions are delicate, around 30 minutes. Mix in port, if utilizing.
3. In the meantime, warm oven with rack in center. Scoop soup into 6-ounce ramekins, then top each with a toasted baguette cut or two. Wrap cheddar on top of bread so it hangs over the edge of the ramekin

marginally. Put ramekins on a rimmed baking sheet and cook until cheddar is browned in spots, around 1/2 minutes. Serve instantly.

44. Wonderful Worms in Dirt

Ingredients

- 8 franks, cut the long way into 1/2-creep thick strips
- 2 (15-ounce) jars dark beans, drained and slashed

Method

1. Heat a large pot of water to the point of boiling over high warmth. Decrease warmth to a stew; include wieners and stew until they start to twist; drain.
2. Put dark beans in a serving dish and top with twisted franks, tenderly tucking them into the beans to give the presence of worms in soil; serve promptly.

45. Best Pickled Brains

Ingredients

- 1 cup red-wine vinegar
- 3 cups white-wine vinegar
- 1 cup sugar
- 1/2 cup salt
- 1 tablespoon dark peppercorns
- 1 tablespoon brown mustard seeds
- 5 or 6 red pearl onions
- 2 to 3 heads cauliflower

Method

1. Put cauliflower in a substantial glass heatproof jug or canister, situating florets against the glass; put aside.
2. Fill a substantial pot with 8 cups water. Include both vinegars, sugar, salt, peppercorns, mustard seeds, and onions. Heat to the point of boiling.
3. Deliberately pour boiling fluid over cauliflower; let cool to room temperature. Cover and exchange to cooler. Let chill overnight or up to 1 week.

HALLOWEEN COOKBOOK

46. Spicy Tasty Bat Wings

Ingredients

- 3 pounds chicken wings (around 16 pieces), washed and tapped dry
- Honey Mustard Sauce
- Hot Sauce for Bat Wings

Method

1. Preheat grill. Lay wings on a rimmed baking sheet, wingtips down. Put under oven, 5 1/2 to 6 inches from warmth source. Sear until brilliant brown and cooked through, turning container as vital, 35 to 40 minutes.
2. Utilizing tongs, expel wings to a substantial bowl. Drain fat from baking sheet into warmth safe bowl, and dispose of.
3. Hurl wings with sauce. Come back to baking sheet, wingtips down. Hold bowl with residual sauce. Put wings under oven, and cook until sauce has coated, 2 to 3 minutes, turning dish once.
4. Return wings to bowl, and hurl to coat. Serve instantly.

Copyright © 2016 – All Rights Reserved | Katya Johansson

KATYA JOHANSSON

47. Wonderful Ghastly Ghoulash

Ingredients

- 2 pounds stew meat, cut into 1-crawl solid shapes
- Coarse salt and newly ground pepper
- 2 tablespoons generally useful flour
- 1/4 cup vegetable oil
- 1 medium onion, cut into 1/4-creep dice
- 3 garlic cloves, minced
- 1/2 cup dry red wine
- 1 tablespoon paprika
- 2 jars (28 ounces each) diced tomatoes
- 2 cups custom made or low-sodium locally acquired hamburger stock
- 2 tablespoons tomato glue
- 2 sprigs crisp oregano, in addition to additional leaves for trimming
- 2 carrots, peeled and cut into 1/4-crawl rounds
- 12 ounces Yukon gold potatoes, peeled and cut into 1-crawl pieces
- 4 ounces thick bacon, cut into 1/4-crawl pieces
- 10 ounces little white mushrooms (quartered assuming huge)
- 1 box (10 ounces) solidified pearl onions, defrosted and drained
- 1 red or green ringer pepper, coarsely cleaved
- Caraway Egg Noodles, for serving

HALLOWEEN COOKBOOK

METHOD

1. Hurl hamburger with salt, pepper, and flour in a medium bowl. Warm 2 tablespoons oil in a large stockpot or Dutch stove over medium-high warmth until hot. Brown portion of hamburger on all sides, 4 to 6 minutes add up to. Exchange hamburger to a plate with an opened spoon. Rehash with residual meat and 2 tablespoons oil.
2. Add onion to fat in pot; cook, mixing every so often, until only delicate, around 3 minutes. Mix in garlic; cook 1 minute. Include wine; cook, blending up brown bits, until most fluid has vanished, around 2 minutes.
3. Return meat to pot. Mix in paprika, tomatoes, stock, tomato glue, and oregano. Season with salt and pepper. Cover; decrease warm. Delicately stew until meat is only delicate, around 1/2 hours.
4. Blend in carrots and potatoes; keep on simmering until vegetables and meat are exceptionally delicate, 20 to 30 minutes.
5. In the meantime, cook bacon in a dry large skillet over medium warmth until fresh, around 5 minutes. Exchange to paper towels to drain. Include mushrooms, pearl onions, and chime pepper to fat in skillet; cook until vegetables are delicate and brilliant brown, and fluid has generally dissipated. Add to goulash.
6. Season goulash with salt and pepper, if vital. Decorate with bacon pieces and oregano. Present with caraway egg noodles.

Copyright © 2016 – All Rights Reserved | Katya Johansson

48. Amazing Recipe

Ingredients

- Arranged natural product, for example, dull plums, grapes, and figs
- Mimolette cheddar
- Garlic Pumpernickel Crisps
- Cheddar Cheese Ball

Method

1. Mastermind all Ingredients on a plate; serve.

HALLOWEEN COOKBOOK

49. Ghost Sandwiches

Ingredients

- 4 cuts Sara Lee Country Potato Bakery Bread
- 4 cuts Sara Lee Baby Swiss Cheese
- 2 cuts Sara Lee Oven Roasted Breast of Turkey
- 2 cuts Sara Lee Virginia Brand Baked Ham
- 3 large eggs
- 1/4 cup milk
- 1/2 teaspoon coarse salt
- 1 tablespoon unsalted margarine
- 1 tablespoon additional virgin olive oil
- Confectioners' sugar, for tidying (Optional)

Method

2. Lay bread cuts on work surface. On 2 bread cuts, put 1 cut cheddar, 1 cut turkey, 1 cut ham, and 1 more cut of cheddar; top each with outstanding bread cut.
3. Utilizing a 5-by-4-creep phantom formed treat cutter, cut out an apparition molded sandwich; rehash with outstanding Ingredients. Put aside.
4. In a shallow dish, whisk together eggs, milk, and salt.
5. In a huge nonstick skillet, warm spread and olive oil over medium-low warmth. Plunge every sandwich in egg blend to coat well on both sides, and place in skillet. Cook, turning once, until brilliant brown and cheddar is softened, around 4 minutes for every side. Serve promptly, tidied with confectioners' sugar, if craved.

KATYA JOHANSSON

50. Eye Catching Soup

Ingredients

- 2 tablespoons unsalted margarine
- 1 onion, finely slashed
- 3 garlic cloves, minced
- 1/2 cup dry white wine
- 2 jars (28 ounces each) squashed tomatoes
- 1 quart custom made or low-sodium locally acquired chicken stock
- 3 sprigs oregano or marjoram
- 1/2 cup creamer
- Coarse salt and crisply ground pepper
- 6 set dark Kalamata olives
- 2 sprigs crisp rosemary
- 4 crisp chives, cut into 1-crawl pieces
- 1 pound (around 30) bocconcini (nibble measure mozzarella balls)
- 1 bump little pimiento-stuffed olives

Method

1. Soften margarine in a huge pan over medium-low warmth. Include onion and garlic, and cook until onion is translucent, around 6 minutes.
2. Include wine, and cook until most fluid has vanished, around 1 minute. Include tomatoes, stock, and oregano,

Copyright © 2016 – All Rights Reserved | Katya Johansson

HALLOWEEN COOKBOOK

and heat to the point of boiling. Lessen warmth, and stew tenderly until thickened, around 45 minutes.
3. Utilizing an opened spoon, expel herbs. Puree soup in little clumps until smooth. Come back to dish, and gradually pour in cream, blending continually. Season with salt and pepper.
4. In the interim, make the bugs: Use a toothpick to puncture each Kalamata olive 4 times (completely through to opposite side). Embed a rosemary leaf into every opening to make eight legs. Embed two bits of chive into the little gap toward the end of the olive to make receiving wires.
5. Make the eyeballs: Using a little melon hotshot, scoop out an opening from each bocconcini. Have every pimiento-stuffed olive across. Put a half, cut side out, in debt in each bocconcini to make eyeballs.
6. Spoon hot soup into shallow dishes. Coast 4 or 5 eyeballs in soup, and place a bug on edge of every bowl.

KATYA JOHANSSON

51. Tasty Creature Chips

Ingredients

- Plain or spread seasoned vegetable-oil cooking spray
- 24 arranged huge flour tortillas, for example, plain, entire wheat, and sun-dried tomato
- Coarse salt
- 3 pounds ready Hass avocados, (around 7), hollowed, peeled, and cut into pieces
- 1/4 cup newly squeezed lime juice, (around 3 limes)
- 1/4 teaspoon newly ground pepper
- 1 new jalapeno chili, seeded and finely slashed
- 1/4 cup cleaved new cilantro, leaves

Method

1. Preheat stove to 350 degrees. Coat a baking sheet with cooking spray. Utilizing a couple Halloween roused treat cutters, cut shapes from tortillas. Organize the greatest number of shapes as can fit in a solitary layer on oiled sheet. Coat tortillas with cooking spray, and season with salt. Prepare until marginally obscured and fresh, 10 to 12 minutes. Exchange to a wire rack to cool. Rehash with outstanding tortilla shapes, utilizing a clean, cooled baking sheet.
2. Put avocados, lime juice, 1/2 teaspoons salt and the pepper, jalapeno, and cilantro in an large bowl. Squash with a fork until stout. Present with chips.

HALLOWEEN COOKBOOK

52. Grilled Cheese Tasty Sandwiches

Ingredients

- 8 cuts cheddar (4-by-4-by-1/8-crawl)
- 8 cuts (1/2-crawl thick) pumpernickel bread
- 4 tablespoons (1/2 stick) unsalted margarine, room temperature
- 4 teaspoons Dijon mustard
- Celery Broomsticks

Method

1. Preheat broiler to 400 degrees. Utilizing a witch's cap treat cutter, cut out a cap from 4 cuts of cheddar; put aside.
2. Spread one side of every cut of bread with margarine. Spread the unbuttered side of 4 cuts of bread with the mustard. Put on a baking sheet, buttered-side down.
3. Partition remaining cheddar, in addition to any scraps, between the cuts of bread on the baking sheet. Best with residual bread, flattered side.
4. Put sandwiches in stove and cook 10 minutes, or until cheddar has dissolved. Put a cheddar cap on top of every sandwich. Heat until simply liquefied, around 2 minutes. Present with celery broomsticks.

Copyright © 2016 – All Rights Reserved | Katya Johansson

53. Amazing Fingers and Toes

Ingredients

- Red or green food shading, (Optional, for fingers)
- 24 whitened almonds, divided the long way
- 2 cups warm water (110 degrees), in addition to 3 quarts, in addition to 1 tablespoon
- 1 tablespoon sugar
- 1 bundle dynamic dry yeast (1/4 ounce)
- Vegetable oil
- 5 to 6 cups universally handy flour, in addition to additional for work surface
- 1 tablespoon coarse salt
- 2 tablespoons baking pop
- 1 large egg
- Ocean salt
- Singed rosemary (Optional, for toes)

Method

1. Put a little measure of food shading, if utilizing, in a shallow bowl, and, utilizing a paintbrush, shading the adjusted side of every split almond; put aside to dry.
2. Empty 2 cups water into the bowl of an electric blender fitted with the mixture snare connection. Include sugar; blend to break up. Sprinkle with yeast, and let remain until yeast starts to bubble, around 5 minutes. Beat in 1 cup flour into yeast on low speed until joined. Beat in

HALLOWEEN COOKBOOK

coarse salt; include 3 1/2 cups flour, and beat until consolidated. Keep beating until mixture pulls far from bowl, 1 to 2 minutes. Include 1/2 cup flour. Beat 1 minute more. On the off chance that mixture is sticky, mean 1 cup more flour. Exchange to a daintily floured surface; massage until smooth, 1 minute.

3. Coat a large bowl with cooking spray. Exchange mixture to bowl, swinging batter to coat with oil. Cover with plastic wrap; let rest in a warm spot to ascend until multiplied in size, around 60 minutes.

4. Preheat broiler to 450 degrees. Heat 3 quarts water to the point of boiling in a 6-quart straight-sided pot over high warmth; decrease to a stew. Include baking pop. Delicately coat two baking sheets with cooking spray. Separate mixture into quarters. Work with one quarter at once, and cover remaining mixture with plastic wrap. Partition first quarter into 12 pieces. On a softly floured work surface, roll every piece forward and backward with your palm framing a long finger shape, around 3 to 4 inches. Pinch batter in two spots to shape knuckles. Then again, to make toes, roll every piece with the goal that it is somewhat shorter and fatter, around 2 inches. Pinch in 1 place to shape the knuckle. At the point when 12 fingers or toes are framed, exchange to stewing water. Poach for 1 minute. Utilizing an opened spoon, exchange fingers to the readied baking sheets. Rehash with outstanding mixture, whitening every arrangement of 12 fingers or toes before making more.

5. Beat egg with 1 tablespoon water. Brush pretzel fingers and toes with the egg wash. Utilizing a sharp blade, gently score every knuckle around three times. Sprinkle with ocean salt and rosemary, if utilizing. Position almond nails, pushing them into batter to connect. Prepare until brilliant brown, 12 to 15 minutes. Let cool on wire rack.

KATYA JOHANSSON

54. Petrified Cheese Log

Ingredients

- 5 ounces blue cheddar
- 5 ounces mollified cream cheddar
- Dark sesame seeds
- Blue food shading (Optional)
- Wafers, for serving

Method

1. Blend blue cheddar with 2 or 3 drops of blue food shading, if wanted; join with relaxed cream cheddar.
2. Move into a log, and wrap in plastic. Refrigerate until firm. Unwrap, and move sign in dark sesame seeds. Present with wafers.

55. Halloween Cheese Crackers

Ingredients

- 4 1/2 ounces Shropshire blue cheddar
- 1/4 cup in addition to 3 tablespoons generally useful flour
- 3 tablespoons cornstarch
- 3 tablespoons unsalted spread, mollified
- 1/8 teaspoon newly ground pepper
- 1/4 teaspoon coarse salt

Method

1. Put all Ingredients in the bowl of a food processor and heartbeat until a mixture has shaped. Exchange batter to work surface and shape into a circle. Wrap in plastic wrap and refrigerate until chilled, no less than 60 minutes.
2. Preheat stove to 375 degrees. Line a baking sheet with material paper or a nonstick baking mat; put aside.
3. Take off batter on a floured work surface to 1/8-crawl thick. Cut batter into fancied shapes utilizing 1/2-to-4-creep treat cutters, rerolling scraps as you go.
4. Exchange mixture to arranged baking sheet. Prepare until fresh and dim orange, 10 to 12 minutes. Exchange wafers to a wire rack to cool.

KATYA JOHANSSON

56. Devils on Wonderful Horseback

Ingredients

- 8 cuts bacon, cut into thirds
- 24 prunes, set

Method

1. Preheat broiler to 400 degrees. Line a huge rimmed baking sheet with thwart. Wrap bacon pieces around prunes and secure with toothpicks.
2. Heat on sheet until bacon is browned, around 15 minutes, flipping part of the way through. Serve warm.

HALLOWEEN COOKBOOK

57. Amazing Tacos

Ingredients

- 1 lb. ground meat
- (1/4 ounce) bundle taco flavoring blend
- 12 taco shells
- 3/4 cup salsa
- 3/4 cup acrid cream
- 1 tomatoes, little 3D shapes
- 1 little head lettuce, cut into little confetti squares
- 1 (2 1/4 ounce) dark olives, cut
- 1 cup cheddar, Shredded and Long

Method

1. Blend meat and flavoring blend. Shape half of the blend into 24 (1-creep) balls; put in 15x10x1-crawl baking container and prepare at 350 F for 15 to 20 minutes or until cooked through.
2. Brown the staying prepared ground hamburger and include salsa.
3. Fill every taco shell with a thin layer of ground hamburger, acrid cream, lettuce, and tomatoes.
4. Position 2 meatballs inside the taco shell and include a dab of sharp cream to each. Embellish with olives to make "eyeballs." Spread the cheddar out along to the top for stringy hair.

Copyright © 2016 – All Rights Reserved | Katya Johansson

58. Amazing Spider Deviled Eggs

Ingredients

- 6 hard-boiled eggs, split
- 3 tablespoons mayonnaise
- 1/2 teaspoon ground mustard
- 1/8 teaspoon salt
- 1/8 teaspoon pepper
- dark olives

Method

1. Sliced eggs down the middle longwise. Slip out yolks and squash.
2. Mix in mayonaise, mustard, salt, and pepper.
3. Sliced entire olive down the middle.
4. Put one half on crushed yolk for the bug's body.
5. Daintily cut the other half for the bug's legs. Put four legs on every side.

59. AMAZING MUMMY DOGS

INGREDIENTS

- 1 (11 ounce) bundle refrigerated breadstick batter (8 number)
- 8 wieners
- mustard
- poppy seed

METHOD

1. Preheat broiler to 375°F Using 1 mixture strip for every, wrap sausage to look like mummies, leaving an opening for eyes.
2. Put on ungreased baking sheet.
3. Heat 12 to 15 minutes or until light brilliant brown.
4. Put dabs of mustard and poppy seeds for eyes and appreciate!

60. Halloween Fingers

Ingredients

- 1 cup unsalted margarine, mellowed
- 1 cup icing sugar (filter through a sifter in the wake of measuring to evacuate bumps)
- 1 vast egg (room temp)
- 1 teaspoon almond separate
- 1 teaspoon vanilla
- 2 1/4 cups universally handy flour
- 1 teaspoon baking powder
- 1 teaspoon salt
- 3/4 cup entire whitened almond (you require around 60)

Method

1. In a blending dish, beat spread sugar, egg and concentrates together.
2. In another blending dish, consolidate flour, baking powder and salt.
3. Beat dry Ingredients into spread blend, then cover bowl and refrigerate for 30 minutes.
4. Preheat stove to 325 degrees F; have treat sheets, fixed with material paper, prepared.
5. Expel just 1/4 of the mixture from fridge (leave rest refrigerated to stay chilly); allot stacking teaspoonful and shape into fingers.
6. Press an almond immovably into the end of each" finger" to make the fingernail.

HALLOWEEN COOKBOOK

7. Underneath the almond and at the inverse end of the finger, press in mixture to make knuckle mostly down; utilizing the back of a table blade, make indents into the knuckle (take a gander at your own particular fingers to get a thought of what this ought to resemble).
8. On the off chance that you need huge monstrous fingers with two contorted knuckles, use around a tbsp of mixture for each treat.
9. Put on paper-lined treat sheets and prepare in preheated stove until a pale brilliant shading - around 20 to 25 minutes.
10. After first sheet goes into the broiler, expel more mixture from the ice chest to make more fingers.
11. At the point when treats are done, expel from broiler and let cool for three minutes.
12. Deliberately lift up almond from every finger and squeeze some red finishing gel onto nail bed, then squeeze almond once again into the right spot; the red gel will creepily overflow out.
13. Exchange to a rack and let cool totally

61. Roasted Healthy Pumpkin Seeds

Ingredients

- 1 cups seeds
- 1/2 cups pumpkin seeds
- 2 teaspoons dissolved margarine (olive oil or vegetable oil function admirably) or 2 teaspoons liquefied oil (olive oil or vegetable oil function admirably)
- salt
- garlic powder (Optional)
- cayenne pepper (Optional)
- flavoring salt (Optional)
- Cajun flavoring (Optional)

Method

1. Preheat stove to 300 degrees F.
2. While it's OK to abandon a few strings and mash on your seeds (it includes season) wipe off any real pieces.
3. Hurl pumpkin seeds in a bowl with the dissolved spread or oil and seasonings of your decision.
4. Spread pumpkin seeds in a solitary layer on baking sheet.
5. Prepare for around 45 minutes, mixing once in a while, until brilliant brown.

HALLOWEEN COOKBOOK

62. HALLOWEEN TASTY FONDUE

INGREDIENTS

- 1 (12 ounce) can dry juice or 1 (12 ounce) can non-hard brew
- 1 lb. sharp Canadian cheddar, ground
- 1 tablespoon cornstarch
- 4 tablespoons mollified spread
- 2 teaspoons dry English-style mustard
- 1 teaspoon Worcestershire sauce
- 1 pinch cayenne pepper
- (1 lb.) loaf heavy entire wheat bread or (1 lb.) loafcrusty rye bread, cut into 1" cubes, cut so every 3D square has a touch of covering and air dry for 2 hours

METHOD

1. Warm the juice or brew to a stew over medium-low warmth.
2. Hurl together the cheddar and the cornstarch.
3. Add cheddar in large modest bunches to the stewing fluid.
4. At the point when the fondue is velvety (you may need to blend once), consolidate the spread, mustard, & Worcestershire and add to the fondue.
5. Blend continually with a wooden spoon until silky& smooth.
6. Season with cayenne and place in a table top fondue dish and place over warmer.

Copyright © 2016 – All Rights Reserved | Katya Johansson

7. Keep the fondue at a delicate stew.

HALLOWEEN COOKBOOK

63. Amazing Yoda Soda

Ingredients

- 3 limes, juice of or 1/4 cup lime juice
- 3 tablespoons sugar
- 1 cup shining water
- 1 scoop lime sherbet or 1 scoop lime sorbet

Method

1. Juice limes to get 1/4 cup lime squeeze (or utilize 1/4 arranged juice!).
2. Consolidate lime squeeze and sugar- - blend to break down sugar.
3. Include shimmering water and blend till blended.
4. Taste and include more sugar if sought.
5. Put sherbet in a tall glass and pour lime blend over top.

Copyright © 2016 – All Rights Reserved | Katya Johansson

KATYA JOHANSSON

64. Apple with Cheese Spread

Ingredients

- 8 ounces cream cheddar (relaxed)
- 1/2 cup harsh cream
- 1 apple (finely slashed)
- 1/4 cup disintegrated blue cheddar
- 1/4 red onion (finely chopped)
- 1/4 cup toasted pecans
- Triscuit wafers (Thins)

Method

1. Beat cream cheddar and sharp cream in bowl.
2. Include apples, blue cheddar, onions and pecans. Blend well.
3. Refrigerate 2 hours.
4. Present with triscuits or a blander tasting saltine.

65. Apple and Blue Cheese Spread

Ingredients

- 8 ounces cream cheddar (diminished)
- 1/2 cup acrid cream
- 1 apple (finely cleaved)
- 1/4 cup disintegrated blue cheddar
- 1/4 red onion (finely chopped)
- 1/4 cup toasted pecans
- Triscuit saltines (Thins)

Method

1. Beat cream cheddar and acrid cream in bowl.
2. Include apples, blue cheddar, onions and pecans. Blend well.
3. Refrigerate 2 hours.
4. Present with triscuits or a blander tasting wafer.